A FIRST LOOK AT AMERICA'S PRESIDENTS

# WILLIAM McKINLEY

## The 25th President

by Diane Bailey

Consultants:
Philip Nash, Associate Professor of History
Pennsylvania State University
Sharon, Pennsylvania

Soo Chun Lu, Associate Professor of History
Indiana University of Pennsylvania
Indiana, Pennsylvania

BEARPORT PUBLISHING

New York, New York

**Credits**

Cover, Courtesy National Portrait Gallery; 4, © North Wind Picture Archives/Alamy; 5, Courtesy Library of Congress; 6, © Classic Stock/Alamy; 7, © Glenn Nagel/Dreamstime; 8, Courtesy Giles County Historical Society; 9T, Courtesy Library of Congress; 9B, © Julie Clopper/Shutterstock; 10, Courtesy Library of Congress; 11R, © Belinka/Dreamstime; 11B, © North Wind Picture Archives/Alamy; 11T, Courtesy National Archives; 12, © Niday Picture Library/Alamy; 13L, Courtesy Library of Congress; 13R, © World History Archive/Alamy; 14, Courtesy Library of Congress; 15, © Historical Art Collection/Alamy; 16, Courtesy Library of Congress; 17T, Courtesy Library of Congress; 17B, Courtesy Library of Congress; 18, © Richard Lowthian/Dreamstime; 19T, © Benkrut/Dreamstime; 19B, © Tadamichi/Dreamstime; 20T, Courtesy Giles County Historical Society; 20B, Courtesy Library of Congress; 21T, Courtesy Library of Congress; 21TR, Courtesy Library of Congress; 21B, © North Wind Picture Archives/Alamy; 22, © James Crawford/Dreamstime; 23T, © Tadamichi/Dreamstime; 23B, Courtesy Giles County Historical Society; 23R, © Niday Picture Library/Alamy.

Publisher: Kenn Goin
Senior Editor: Joyce Tavolacci
Creative Director: Spencer Brinker
Production and Photo Research: Shoreline Publishing Group LLC

*Library of Congress Cataloging-in-Publication Data*

Names: Bailey, Diane, 1966– author. | Nash, Philip, consultant.
Title: William McKinley: the 25th President / by Diane Bailey ; consultant, Philip Nash, Associate Professor of History, Pennsylvania State University.
Description: New York, New York : Bearport Publishing, [2017] | Series: A first look at America's presidents | Includes bibliographical references and index. | Audience: Ages 6–10.
Identifiers: LCCN 2016012092 (print) | LCCN 2016012661 (ebook) | ISBN 9781944102685 (library binding) | ISBN 9781944997373 (ebook)
Subjects: LCSH: McKinley, William, 1843-1901—Juvenile literature. | Presidents—United States—Biography—Juvenile literature.
Classification: LCC E711.6 .B26 2017 (print) | LCC E711.6 (ebook) | DDC 973.8/8092—dc23
LC record available at http://lccn.loc.gov/2016012092

For more information, write to Bearport Publishing Company, Inc., 45 West 21st Street, Suite 3B, New York, New York 10010. Printed in the United States of America.

10 9 8 7 6 5 4 3 2 1

# CONTENTS

**Changing Times** . . . . . . . . . . . . . . . **4**

**Ohio Boy** . . . . . . . . . . . . . . . . . . . **6**

**A Brave Soldier** . . . . . . . . . . . . . . **8**

**Government Work** . . . . . . . . . . . **10**

**Listening to the People** . . . . . . . **12**

**A Popular President** . . . . . . . . . . **14**

**A Last Handshake** . . . . . . . . . . . . **16**

**Remembering McKinley** . . . . . . . **18**

Timeline . . . . . . . . . . . . . . . . . . . 20

Facts and Quotes . . . . . . . . . . . . . . 22

Glossary . . . . . . . . . . . . . . . . . . . 23

Index . . . . . . . . . . . . . . . . . . . . . 24

Read More . . . . . . . . . . . . . . . . . . 24

Learn More Online . . . . . . . . . . . . . 24

About the Author . . . . . . . . . . . . . . 24

# Changing Times

Wherever President William McKinley went, cheering crowds greeted him. He was a **popular** and strong leader. He fought to make the United States into a world power. He also helped American businesses grow.

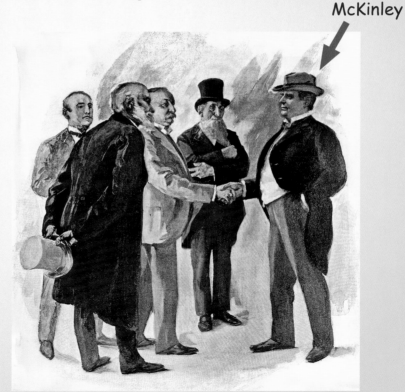
McKinley

McKinley was known for his fast handshake. People called it "the McKinley grip."

William McKinley was the 25th president. He served from 1897 to 1901.

5

# Ohio Boy

William McKinley was born in Ohio in 1843. He was the seventh of eight children. Young William always had a lot of friends. In school, he worked hard and dreamed of becoming a teacher.

As a boy, William liked to ride horses, swim, and fly kites.

In William's day, children often went swimming in ponds or lakes.

William attended a one-room schoolhouse like this one.

# A Brave Soldier

In 1861, when William was 18 years old, the Civil War began. He joined the Army to help the **Union**. At the Battle of Antietam (an-TEE-tuhm), William risked his life to bring food to hungry soldiers. He received a medal for his bravery.

The Civil War was fought between the Northern states and the Southern states. It lasted from 1861 to 1865.

McKinley in his Union Army uniform

The Northern states were also called the Union. The Union fought to keep the country together and to end slavery.

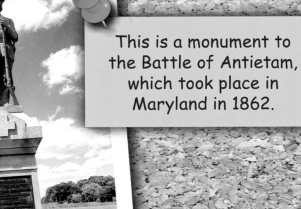

This is a monument to the Battle of Antietam, which took place in Maryland in 1862.

After the war, McKinley worked as a lawyer. In 1876, he was **elected** to the U.S. House of Representatives. To help American businesses, he introduced a **tariff** on products from other countries. As a result, the price of **foreign** goods rose. Therefore, people bought more American products. This helped U.S. businesses grow.

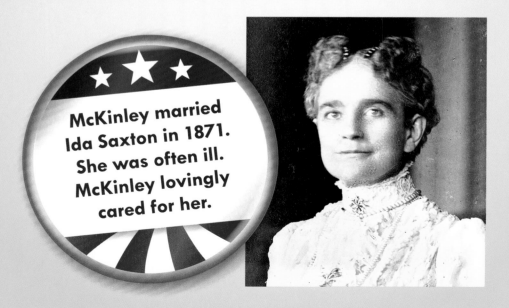

McKinley married Ida Saxton in 1871. She was often ill. McKinley lovingly cared for her.

McKinley's tariff made foreign goods, such as wheat, more expensive. Wheat grown in America was cheaper, so people bought more of it.

THE COMMERCIAL POLICY
OF THE
BRITISH COLONIES
AND
THE McKINLEY TARIFF

BY
EARL GREY, K.G., G.C.M.G.

Presented
BY THE

London
MACMILLAN AND CO.
AND NEW YORK
1892

# Listening to the People

In 1891, McKinley ran for governor of Ohio—and won. As governor, he helped working people. He introduced laws that gave railroad workers more rights. He also made new rules to stop child **labor**. McKinley became very popular. In 1896, he decided to run for president. He won by 600,000 votes!

When McKinley was governor, many children worked long hours in factories. McKinley set up laws to help protect child workers.

A poster from McKinley's 1896 presidential run

When McKinley ran for president, he often gave speeches from his front porch.

# A Popular President

As president, McKinley worked to make the United States more powerful. In 1898, he led a war to free Cuba from Spanish rule. After five months, America won the war and took control of Cuba, Puerto Rico, and other Spanish **colonies**.

In 1900, McKinley was reelected president.

Theodore Roosevelt fought in the 1898 conflict, which was called the Spanish-American War. He then became McKinley's vice president in 1901.

This illustration shows a battle during the Spanish-American War.

15

# A Last Handshake

In September 1901, McKinley attended a huge fair in Buffalo, New York. He gave a speech and then shook hands with people in the crowd. One man was holding a gun. He shot McKinley in the stomach. A week later, McKinley died.

The fair in Buffalo where McKinley was shot

The man who shot McKinley was named Leon Czolgosz.

Leon Czolgosz

After McKinley was shot, he asked his guards not to hurt Leon Czolgosz.

Theodore Roosevelt became president after McKinley died.

# Remembering McKinley

Americans were saddened by McKinley's death. He was a popular president. Under his leadership, the country became a strong world power.

Denali, a mountain in Alaska, is also known as Mount McKinley. It was named after President McKinley.

President McKinley is buried in this tomb in Canton, Ohio.

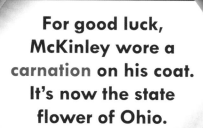

For good luck, McKinley wore a **carnation** on his coat. It's now the state flower of Ohio.

# TIMELINE

Here are some
major events from
William McKinley's life.

## 1843
William McKinley is
born in Niles, Ohio.

## 1862
McKinley fights
at the Battle
of Antietam.

1840     1850     1860     1870

## 1861–1865
The Civil War

## 1896
McKinley is
elected President.

## 1900
McKinley is reelected for
a second term as president.

## 1877–1891
McKinley serves in the U.S.
House of Representatives.

## 1901
McKinley is
killed in office.

| 1880 | 1890 | 1900 | 1910 |

## April 1898–
## August 1898
The Spanish-American War

## 1891
McKinley is elected
governor of Ohio.

"That's all a man can hope for during his lifetime—to set an example."

"The free man cannot be long an ignorant man."

McKinley served in the Civil War with his friend Rutherford B. Hayes, who was president from 1877 to 1881.

McKinley had a pet parrot. It could whistle the song "Yankee Doodle."

"Wars should never be entered upon until every agency of peace has failed."

# GLOSSARY

**carnation** (kahr-NAY-shuhn)  a type of plant with gray-green leaves and large flowers

**colonies** (KOL-uh-neez)  areas that have been settled by people from another country and are ruled by that country

**elected** (ee-LEK-ted)  to be chosen by a vote

**foreign** (FORE-ihn)  from outside the country

**labor** (LAY-bur)  hard physical work

**popular** (POP-yuh-lur) liked by many people

**tariff** (TAR-if)  a tax charged on goods that are imported or exported

**Union** (YOON-yun)  the Northern states during the U.S. Civil War

# Index

Battle of Antietam 8–9, 20
Buffalo, New York 16
childhood 6–7
Civil War 8, 20
Cuba 14
Czolgosz, Leon 16

elections 12
House of Representatives
   10, 20
Mount McKinley (Denali) 18
Ohio 6, 12, 18, 20
Roosevelt, Theodore 14, 17

Saxton, Ida 10
Spain 14
Spanish-American War
   14–15, 21
tariffs 10–11
workers 10, 12

# Read More

**Amoroso, Cynthia.** *William McKinley: Our Twenty-Fifth President (Presidents of the U.S.A.).* North Mankato, MN: The Child's World (2008).

**Gunderson, Megan M.** *William McKinley: 25th President of the United States (United States Presidents).* Minneapolis, MN: ABDO (2009).

**Venezia, Mike.** *William McKinley: Twenty-Fifth President, 1897–1901 (Getting to Know U.S. Presidents).* Danbury, CT: Children's Press (2006).

# Learn More Online

To learn more about William McKinley, visit
**www.bearportpublishing.com/AmericasPresidents**

About the Author:
Diane Bailey has
written dozens
of books for kids.
She lives in Kansas.